# SNOW PLAY

# SNOW PLAY

## HOW TO MAKE

## FORTS & SLIDES & WINTER CAMPFIRES

### THE PLUS COOLEST
### LOCH NESS MONSTER

AND * 23 * OTHER BRRRILLIANT
PROJECTS IN THE SNOW

Birgitta Ralston

ARTISAN

Published by Artisan
A Division of Workman Publishing Company, Inc.
225 Varick Street
New York, NY 10014-4381
www.artisanbooks.com

Library of Congress Control Number: 2010930866

ISBN: 978-1-57965-405-4

Concept & project design by Birgitta Ralston
Graphic design by Nick Caruso
Illustrations by Dana Stimming

Printed in China

First printing, December 2010

10 9 8 7 6 5 4 3 2 1

DISCLAIMER

Many of the projects described in this book
could be dangerous to build. The publisher
and author disclaim responsibility for any loss,
injury, or damages caused as a result of any of
the instructions described in this book.

To the Ralston & Bau team, whose talent,
inspiration, and raw muscle power made this a
final result to be proud of.

# CONTENTS

# INTRODUCTION

**You wake up to a landscape changed beyond recognition.** Everything is buried underneath a thick blanket of snow. Familiar objects have been changed into strange shapes; all that is left is a clean, white surface beckoning to you to come outside.

Anyone who has experienced a scenario like this will relate to the creative forces triggered by snow. Just look at how spontaneously children play and build with snow. It invites us to create, and to use our entire bodies in doing so—pushing, throwing, packing, digging, lifting, and carving! Snow represents fun and creativity—and it's all for free!

The idea for this book came about a few years ago. After a move to Paris, my new European city life made me long for the Nordic country where I was raised. Being so

accustomed to snow, when it was no longer part of my daily life, I discovered a new appreciation for its beauty. Living in Paris meant I was fortunate to have snow within close reach. Yet some scientists predict that by 2050 the Alps in central Europe—home to numerous skiing resorts—will be without snow. Our climate is the frame and the outer boundary of everything we do, and if it should change, it will in turn change our lives. This book is about cherishing snow, having fun and creating something with it. I believe that if we become more at one with our environment and celebrate it, we will also find ways to protect it.

Snow is a wonderful material; it's easy to work with and shape. In most regions of the world where we find naturally occurring snow, there are strong traditions of utilizing this amazing material, for instance, in building a shelter (see Snow Cave, page 101). In modern times, snow sculpting has become much more of a fanciful art, and there is no limit to the things you can build with it (see Pixelman, page 26). Some traditional snow sculptures have survived the test of time, and yet there are still new ways to create our old favorites (see Funky Snowmen, page 41). However you choose to play in the snow, it should bring you fun and relaxation. When you're ready to compete (or just enjoy the work of other snow enthusiasts!), a range of annual festivals, events, and competitions celebrate the art of shaping snow and ice. If you'd like to see the work of the pros for yourself, you'll find a listing of festival cities in the back of this book (page 105).

There is something beautiful about the limited time span of snow. After all, when the temperature rises, whatever you've built might be gone by the following day. This encourages us to build rapidly and get quick results, since we know it cannot last forever. Take photographs of your work– that's the only way you can ensure it endures! You might even consider keeping a journal of the projects you've built, noting when you built them and who was involved. It's a great way to create a memory of your snow adventures.

Be inspired by the ideas and projects presented in this book, try something new, and have fun in the process. The wonderful thing is that you don't need to be a professional to create beautiful things from snow—snow makes us all instant sculptors. This book is here to get you started.

# HOW TO USE THIS BOOK

## Learning comes from doing, so get out there and explore!

Specific snow-building techniques and the tools needed for each project are listed in the next several pages. We attempted to use only tools that are readily available in your home or are at least easy enough to purchase at a nearby store. There are projects here for people of all abilities—and all ages, too. If you have a large group of people, try tackling one of the larger projects, like the Winter Campfire (page 50), the Snowball Challenge (page 82), or the Spiral Yeti (page 88). If you're playing in the snow with young children, try one of the projects on a smaller scale, like Snowball Lantern (page 59), White Angel (page 77), or Curious Footprints (page 70).

## Tools and Materials

For some of the projects in this book, you'll need nothing but your hands and muscle power; for others, you'll need some specific tools. We tried to create these projects using items that are part of every household, but remember, snow is an easy material to work with.

If you don't own the tool described, substitute. A standard plastic bucket can be replaced by other plastic molds—even a rectangular ice cream container or a porcelain bowl. An LED bulb can be replaced with a tea light or candle. And all the decorative materials mentioned in the projects are just waiting for customization. Use your imagination!

Always remember that some tools, such as saws and knives, can harm you—and others—so use them carefully. Children should only use these tools under the supervision of an adult.

scissors

weight or stone

shovel

box cutter

rectangular bucket

paper & pen

stick

probe

round bucket

bucket

drinking glass

screwdriver

matches

spray bottle

rope

brick maker

snowball maker

watering can

japanese saw

cookie cutters

stopwatch

small hand shovel

container

ice cube tray

knife

saw

## TOOLS

BRICK MAKER A brick maker can be purchased in toy stores or online, and is a tool created specifically to make snow bricks. The standard brick maker is 6 by 12 inches (15 cm by 30 cm) and has a handle. If you cannot find one, many everyday household objects will do just as well. Use plastic storage boxes of various sizes, an empty ice cream tub, molds from the sandbox, or an old cake pan.

BUCKET Use a round 10-quart (9.5 liter) standard water bucket for mixing snow and as a mold to make large building blocks.

BUCKET (RECTANGULAR) Use a large-size plastic bucket approximately 16½ by 12 by 14 inches (42 by 30 by 35 cm) for mixing snow, and as a mold to make large building blocks.

BUCKET (ROUND) For a large-size bucket about 20 inches in diameter by 13½ inches in height (50 by 34 cm), soft plastic is preferable. It's

more flexible than hard plastic and will not break if water or snow freezes inside it. Use for mixing snow, carrying snow, and as a mold for making large building blocks.

CONTAINER OR VARIOUS PLASTIC MOLDS Use small plastic molds and containers in various sizes: sandbox buckets, storage boxes, and empty food tubs all work well.

COOKIE CUTTERS Cookie cutters can be used to cut various decorations into the preferred shape.

DRINKING GLASS Use a standard drinking cup: size and color are unimportant, but plastic is best.

HAND SHOVEL Use either a plastic sand shovel from the beach or sandbox or a small garden spade to carve fine detail into mounds of snow, to compress snow into molds, to smooth surfaces, and to stir water into snow to make it sticky.

ICE CUBE TRAY Several varieties of ice cube trays are available, including trays that give the cubes fancy shapes. Look for silicone ones to make ice cube removal easier.

JAPANESE SAW The Japanese saw has a conical blade and is used to make fine, detailed cuts. The very thin and flexible blade can be used for delicate work on ice projects.

KNIFE You should be able to make all these projects having two standard knives on hand: a box cutter, to cut paper and cardboard; and a small knife, to slice vegetables and cut out decorations, etc.

MATCHES Storm matches are preferred since they're weatherproof and should work even in wet surroundings. Long matches are useful, as they burn longer and are easier to handle with gloved fingers. Instead of matches you can use a long-reach butane lighter, which is the safest way to light a wick or a fireplace.

PAPER AND PEN It is a good idea to draw your designs on paper before you head outside. Use paper to make stencils, too. If you want to take a drawing outside, place it inside a plastic sleeve to protect the paper from getting wet.

PROBE A probe is a professional tool used in winter rescue and mountaineering. It is a collapsible metal stick. Use a probe to test snow thickness and depth.

ROPE Use string, rope, or twine, depending on the project. Find whatever you have handy that seems appropriate.

SAW A handheld wood saw is fairly light and short, useful for cutting details as well as general shaping. The blade is thicker and stiffer than the one on a Japanese saw. It's great for cutting out building blocks and making narrow, straight lines in the snow as well as making sharp angles and squaring off corners in hard or compressed snow.

**SCISSORS** A pair of scissors can be used to snip string or to cut out shapes from paper, cardboard, or polystyrene.

**SCREWDRIVER** Use any type of screwdriver to pierce holes in paper, cardboard, polystyrene, and other materials.

**SHOVEL** You can use a long-handled metal shovel or a larger snow shovel. A snow shovel, usually made of plastic or aluminium, is lightweight. Use it for clearing areas of snow, filling buckets, making and compressing mounds of snow, and patting the ground smooth. This tool clears an area quickly, but be careful about lifting too much snow at once.

**SNOWBALL MAKER** The snowball maker is a plastic snowball mold, which can be bought in toy stores or online. However, the usual way to make snowballs is with your hands, pressing snow together between your palms and shaping it into a sphere.

**SPRAY BOTTLE** A standard spray bottle for watering plants can also be used for snow sculpting. Be aware that the nozzle might freeze if the temperature is very cold.

**STICK** A straight, firm, and relatively long item, such as a stick or a ruler, can be used in projects that call for measuring.

**STOPWATCH** Have a stopwatch on hand to time contestants in competitions. Most mobile phones come equipped with such a timer.

**WATERING CAN** A watering can is a helpful tool for making sticky snow or when you have to "glue" blocks of snow together, as it evenly sprinkles a controlled amount of water where you need it.

**WEIGHT OR STONE** For a weight, you can use anything heavy, such as a stone, a big log of firewood, or a brick. Make sure the weight is waterproof: a book might be heavy enough, but it would be damaged by the wet snow.

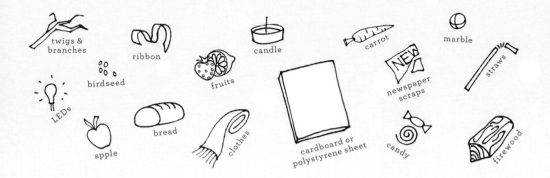

twigs & branches

ribbon

candle

carrot

marble

birdseed

fruits

newspaper scraps

straws

LEDs

bread

clothes

cardboard or polystyrene sheet

candy

firewood

apple

## MATERIALS

In all projects we have tried to use materials that are biodegradable whenever possible, to not leave garbage in nature when the snow melts.

**APPLE** Choose apples with a beautiful red or green color; and remember to bring a few to snack on afterward!

**BIRDSEED** Birdseed comes in different varieties. In addition to being a great decoration, you'll provide some hungry birds with a good meal. Look for birdseed balls that are easy to hang from a branch.

**BREAD** Use slices of dark, whole-grain bread, which will contrast with the white snow.

**CANDLE** Use tea lights, storm candles, or regular candles. Storm candles will burn even in windy weather and last from 4 to 6 hours. Tea lights and standard candles can be used only in calm weather, or if they are protected by walls of snow.

**CANDY** Any candy with a bright color will look great against the snow. Licorice and other soft candy will bleed color into the snow surrounding it, so these are an excellent choice for giving snow creatures scary eyes with colored rings around them.

**CARDBOARD OR POLYSTYRENE SHEET** Use thick cardboard, at least ¼ inch (6 mm) thick, or sheets of polystyrene. If you don't have them handy, you can buy either one in arts-and-crafts stores.

**CARROT** The best carrots to use are thick and long, so that they stand out against the snow. Baby carrots could be used as variations for tiny snowmen or as decoration on other projects.

**CLOTHES** Mittens, scarves, hats, boots—any clothing worn in cold weather can be used as decoration for snow creatures.

**FIREWOOD** If you don't have a stash of firewood at home, it can be purchased at most gas stations or in supermarkets. The wood needs to be dry in order to light easily.

FRUITS You can use all kinds of fruits and berries to decorate: blueberries, raspberries, lemons, limes, and strawberries are just some suggestions.

LEDS These lights are available from some supermarkets and lighting and arts-and-crafts stores. They are small and come in many different colors. Normally you can buy them ready to use, mostly embedded in a plastic case, or as single bulbs, which you have to attach to a battery.

MARBLE Any type of marble, plastic, or glass—small or big—can be used. They can be any color other than white to make them easier to see in the snow.

NEWSPAPER SCRAPS You'll need some newspaper scraps to light a fire. Place the paper underneath the wood logs, and light it first. Paper burns fast, so handle it carefully and keep a safe distance. Instead of newspaper, you could also use lighting bricks.

RIBBON Ribbons come in many styles, widths, and colors. Choose the one you like the most. If you don't have ribbon at home, you can use any kind of string, twine, or thick thread.

STRAWS Colored drinking straws, preferably with a bend, will add some zip to your snow sculptures. Use a pair of scissors to cut shorter pieces.

TWIGS AND BRANCHES Twigs and branches of various sizes are used as decoration for several projects. Try to use twigs you find already on the ground instead of breaking them off living trees.

## Time Frame

It is not always easy to determine the correct time frame for a project, as this may vary according to elements such as weather, snow quality, number of people, age, experience, and physical strength, but we've given a best estimate for each project.

**15 minutes:** Almost immediate, no more than a few minutes depending on the participants

**Half an hour:** Quite quick, could range from 15 to 40 minutes

**One hour:** Quick, could range from 40 to 90 minutes

**Half a day:** Somewhat time-consuming, approximately 2½ to 4 hours, including breaks

**All day:** Quite time-consuming, approximately 5 to 7 hours, including breaks

**Overnight:** From nighttime to the next day, or about that length of time, to freeze

## Difficulty

The snowflake scale will help you determine the difficulty level of each project. Some are very easy and suitable even for young children; others are more advanced and demand some experience.

✱ Very easy and quick, suitable for everyone, even the smallest children

✱✱ Easy, requires a little more effort and/or time

✱✱✱ Advanced, requires some skill

✱✱✱✱ Very advanced, extensive experience required; seek the advice of professionals

## Type of Work

Each project includes a designation for the type of work required. Keep in mind that some projects combine several types of work. In these cases, the main type is listed first.

BODYWORK Using your entire body with pushing, carrying, and lifting required.

BUILDING/BLOCK Working with blocks of snow—making them, stacking them, and sticking them together—to create a larger structure.

ROLLING/BALL Rolling snowballs of various sizes and stacking them together to form a structure.

SCULPTING/HANDWORK Using your hands or sometimes a hand shovel to shape and/or carve a sculpture.

FOOT/WALKING Walking on or in snow to create a project.

ICE Working with water that is left to freeze—either in a freezer or outside—for several hours or overnight.

## Types of Snow

Snow exists in a variety of densities, qualities, and textures. It can be silkily smooth and powdery with fine crystals; it can be heavy, thick, and sticky like clay; or it can be rock-hard and solid enough for you to walk on top of without falling through. The most obvious factor that affects the snow is temperature, but wind, sun, and climate are also important.

The two types of snow most useful for building snow sculptures and creating snow designs are sticky snow and compressed snow. For snow tracks and games, fresh or powdery snow is the perfect material.

FRESH SNOW is newly fallen; it is very soft, smooth, and perfectly white. Fresh snow is perfect for leaving tracks in, but also to make snowballs, slides, and sculptures if the snow isn't too cold. Fresh snow has not yet been compressed by gravity, therefore it contains a lot of air trapped between the snow crystals. It's more difficult to shape this type of snow into detailed sculptures. Parts could easily break off due to the weaker consistency.

STICKY SNOW occurs naturally when temperatures are just above the freezing point. Many of the projects in this book demand sticky snow, as it is by far the easiest kind to work with when sculpting. Sticky snow feels quite moist, and it's heavier than fresh, powdery snow and easy to shape into snowballs just by using your hands. Also, designs in sticky snow will keep their shape without cracking or breaking apart, making this type of snow perfect for building sculptures that you shape by hand (including snowmen constructed from snowballs of various sizes).

COMPRESSED SNOW occurs when the snow is quite old, especially if the temperature has risen—letting the snow melt slightly—and then fallen again, which makes the snow refreeze. Compressed snow is invaluable for projects using solid blocks of snow that will retain their shape when carved. To cut blocks out of compressed snow, use a hand saw to make a square and then lift the block out using a snow shovel. Compressed snow blocks are perfect for building larger structures that need to be stable and/or angular.

LOOSE, POWDERY SNOW is found at very cold temperatures, when the snow is still reasonably fresh. It can be drizzled or poured into cracks between building blocks to fill them up. It can also be used to erase those last few lumps and bumps, discolored spots, or dirty snow in your project: just take a handful of loose snow and rub it very lightly all over the sculpture while wearing a pair of synthetic mittens or gloves. Your sculpture will look radiantly white, flawless, and smooth.

DEEP SNOW The amount of snow on the ground must be at least 18 inches (50 cm) to consider it "deep." When a project is particularly large in scope, it is best to work with deep snow. This will keep you from having to cart buckets of snow to the building site. Deep snow also allows for more dramatic and visible tracks.

ICE is frozen water, used in this book to create frozen treats and sculptures. You can find ice blocks made by nature, but the easiest way to work with ice is to make it yourself either by putting water in a freezer or leaving it outside when the temperature is well below 32°F (0°C).

CRYSTALLIZED SNOW occurs when the weather turns very cold and dry after fresh snow has fallen. The temperature drop causes the snow to become crystallized. It's as if you can see each individual snow crystal on the snow surface, and when touched it makes a beautiful tinkling sound like the shattering of thin glass. We do not recommend using crystallized snow for sculpting, but it's perfect for making beautiful glistening tracks.

# Techniques

Snow is a magical material. It sticks together, without any glue, as its molecules merge. Snow can easily be formed and shaped; it's one of the most flexible materials on earth! It does not take much experience or know-how to work with snow: just get into a pile of the fluffy white stuff and get started. Every romp in the snow offers an opportunity to learn a new technique, and every project can become a surprising adventure. The following information will help you learn different ways to build with snow.

## GETTING STARTED: PREPARE YOUR LOCATION

When starting a snow project, it's important to begin by choosing a location—usually a flat piece of land with a good amount of snow. Mark your area by tracing its outline in the snow with a shovel, and then clear the area if needed. When you need a circular working area, you can either just make a round shape by eye or a perfect circle with a compass (see page 19)—it's entirely up to you.

## MAKING A BASE OR A MOUND

Most of the sculptures in this book start with building a base or mound as a basic structure. Make a mound of snow either by using a large bucket as a mold or by gathering a pile of snow by hand. If using a mold, simply pack snow into it with a shovel or your hands, compress the snow by pushing it down, and keep adding snow. You will be able to flip the bucket over and turn out a dense cone of snow. You may need to tap the bottom of the bucket to release the cone. The process is similar if you gather a pile of snow by hand: Pile the snow, compress it by patting it with a shovel or your hands, and then add more snow and compress again. Repeat this until you have a mound in the size you need.

## ROLLING A SNOWBALL

Make a regular snowball by gathering snow in your hands and patting it together into a ball. Place the snowball on the snow-covered ground and gently roll it along. As it rolls, more snow will cling to it, making the snowball grow. Carefully pat the snowball as you roll it, to make the new snow stick and change directions as you move along to give it an even shape. You can roll the snowball as large as you like, but it will be difficult to get it much bigger than about thigh-high. Finished snowballs are heavy and tough to move, so plan ahead to end up approximately where you want the snowball to be.

## MAKING STICKY SNOW

If the snow is too fine and powdery or too dry to build with, you can easily make your own sticky snow with the help of a large bucket and a little water. Make sticky snow by adding water from a watering can (just a little at a time) and stirring it into the loose snow with a hand shovel until it's an even consistency. You can make smaller amounts of sticky snow in a small bucket using the same technique.

## MAKING COMPRESSED SNOW

Almost any type of snow can be made hard and dense by compression, which squeezes the air out of it, crushing the snow crystals together. The snow will become compressed if stomped on for a long time, providing it is deep enough (you'll need at least 3 feet [1 m] of snow). When starting with loose, fine snow, be prepared for the process to take a while, but eventually you will be able to cut neat, solid cubes from your compressed snow.

## USING MOLDS

Use a mold to make snow bricks or other shapes such as cones and balls. The best molds for snow sculpting are made from soft plastic. They are rigid enough to allow you to pack the snow to get compact results, and they also release the snow easily. Use a small hand shovel or your hands to add the snow to the mold. When working with molds, you need to use sticky snow (see page 16).

## MAKING A COMPASS

A compass is used to make a perfect circle, which can be useful for many of these projects. You can make your own compass with a wooden pole (for instance, the handle of a snow shovel), a piece of rope, and a saw. The pole should be longer than the depth of the snow. The length of the rope can be variable, but as a guideline, consider that the length of the rope will be identical to the radius of the circle (five feet [1.5 m] is a good place to start). Tie one end of the rope to the pole and the other to the saw. Insert the pole into the snow, into what

will be the center point of your circle, and draw a circle by making a line through the snow with the saw, keeping the rope tight at all times.

## BUILDING WITH BLOCKS

When you build a sculpture from blocks of hard, compressed snow, you might occasionally need to attach a block that protrudes from the sculpture and is only half-supported (if at all) from below. In such cases, it is possible to use water as glue to make sure your structure holds. Simply dribble water from a watering can onto the surfaces you want to stick together, and then hold the pieces in place until they have set. This may take a little time, and works best in cold temperatures.

## MAKING BLOCKS OF SNOW STICK TOGETHER

Often, snow will stick together simply by stacking blocks or cones. To strengthen the structure of the projects, use extra snow to fill in any gaps or cracks between the blocks or cones. If you're building on a very cold day, you may find it difficult to stick blocks together. Try placing one block at a time and letting it "bake" in the sun for 20 to 30 minutes before proceeding with your project. This will melt the snow crystals slightly, effectively gluing the blocks together.

## CARVING

To remove snow from a sculpture to make the shape you want, use your fingers, a small hand shovel, or a Japanese saw to get the details you require.

# SNOW SAFETY

### When going out in the snow . . .

* Plan your trip and check the geographical and weather conditions; places that are safe in the summer are not always safe in winter.
* Always tell someone where you plan to go and when you expect to be back.
* Drink plenty of water and eat some food before going out, as playing in the snow can be very tiring.

### What to Take with You

* A cellular phone with emergency numbers stored in the phone book.
* Extra snacks and drinks. Some quick energy boosters are raisins, nuts, oranges and other fruits, sandwiches filled with protein, hot cocoa, and water.
* Extra layers of clothing in case you become cold or your clothes get wet.

* When going on long outings or high into the mountains, you should take these essential items: topographic map, compass, fire starter, storm matches, first aid kit, flashlight or headlamp with extra batteries, small shovel, emergency shelter and/or sleeping bag, portable probe, and avalanche beacon.

### What to Wear

* Dress warmly, wearing several layers and paying special attention to your ears, fingers, and toes. Woolen clothing is warmer than clothes made from other fabrics such as cotton.
* Outerwear should be waterproof. Wear brightly colored clothing, as this will make you easily visible in the snow.
* Wear waterproof shoes with nonslip soles.
* Wear an oil-based sunscreen, as snow reflects sunlight, making your skin burn very easily.

PAGE 26

We are all familiar with Frosty, but have you met his friends? There's **PIXELMAN,** a funky, urban guy with angular good looks from snow bricks; **MUTATED SNOWMAN,** unlike any Frosty you remember; the coiling **CHILLED NESSIE;** and tiny **FROZEN CREATURES** on extra-long legs.

PAGE 41

PAGE 30

Check out **UPSIDE-DOWN MAN**—he took a headfirst dive into the pile of fresh snow. Follow the instructions for our king-size **LOOK-ALIKES,** and you can produce a likeness of your friends and family members in snow.

PAGE 33

PAGE 38

For purists at heart, we've created a modern twist with **FUNKY SNOWMEN.** Our makeovers turn him into a bunny, a sleepyhead, and one snowman that's made for the birds! Together they're an impressive gang of curious snow creatures!

PAGE 36

PAGE 44

# Pixelman

Pixelman is perfect to build on a clear, cold day when the finished result will freeze to crisp, industrial perfection.

## DID YOU KNOW?

Some North American Inuit call the northern lights *aqsarniit* ("soccer trails") and believe they are the spirits of the dead playing soccer with the head of a walrus.

TIME FRAME **HALF A DAY**

DIFFICULTY ✸✸✸

TYPE **BUILDING/BLOCK**

TYPE OF SNOW **VERY FINE AND COLD**

PEOPLE **2+**

TOOLS

**①**

Using a small hand shovel, fill a rectangular plastic mold with snow (see Techniques, page 19). Be sure to fill the mold completely to keep brick corners intact. Place the brick where you want it and slide the mold carefully off. Continue this process, making and placing one brick at a time.

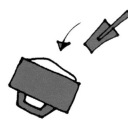

**②**

Form the base by making two identical columns four bricks tall. These two towers should be exactly two brick lengths apart. When completed, Pixelman will stand 13 bricks high (including a base of the first four levels), about as tall as an adult.

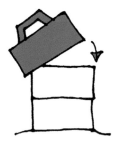

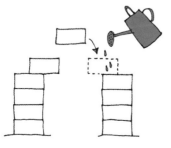

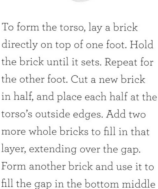

 **3**

To make feet, place one brick so that half is on the tower and half is suspended over the gap between the two base towers. Use water to stick the bricks together. Hold the brick in place until the water freezes. Then repeat the process on the other base.

 **4**

To form the torso, lay a brick directly on top of one foot. Hold the brick until it sets. Repeat for the other foot. Cut a new brick in half, and place each half at the torso's outside edges. Add two more whole bricks to fill in that layer, extending over the gap. Form another brick and use it to fill the gap in the bottom middle layer, holding it until set.

**5**

To form the arms, place a brick of snow at one end of the torso so that half the brick is suspended to the side; hold it there until it freezes in place. Repeat this at the other end of the torso, and then fill the space between the arms with two more bricks.

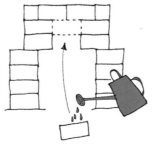

For the T-shaped mouth, put two bricks about a quarter-brick in from the torso's sides, with a half-brick gap in between. Then place a half brick atop each end of this layer. For the next row, place a brick to hang over the gap between the half bricks; hold in place until set, then repeat, leaving a half-brick gap. To make eyes, place half a brick on top of and aligned with the last row's edge. Repeat on the other side, and then lay one full brick centered between them (leaving slits for eyes), bridging the gap over the layer below it.

To finish the mouth, fill the half-brick gap under the center brick, holding it in place until it sets. To complete the eyes, top the half brick with a full brick; repeat on the other side, then place a half brick in the center.

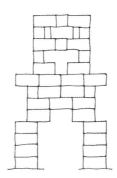

If some bricks stick out a little, use the handsaw to make Pixelman completely even-looking. Repair nicks and broken corners carefully, using a bit of sticky snow to fill gaps between the bricks. Finally, carefully rub Pixelman all over with fine, powdery snow to give him a sharp and flawless finish.

# Chilled Nessie

Many people claim to have seen the Loch Ness monster, but for some reason no one can ever manage to get her on camera. Our snowy version is much easier to catch!

## DID YOU KNOW?

Salt water freezes at a colder temperature than fresh water. This is the reason why lakes freeze over more easily than the ocean, and it is also why we spread salt on the roads during winter.

TIME FRAME **HALF A DAY**

DIFFICULTY ✳✳

TYPE **SCULPTING/ HANDWORK**

TYPE OF SNOW **DEEP AND STICKY**

PEOPLE **3+**

TOOLS

**1**

Locate a spot for your monster, which will be about 23 feet (7 m) long when complete. Using a shovel, fill a large bucket (at least 20 quarts/19 l) with snow. Compress the snow tightly into the bucket; add more snow, and compress it again. Flip the bucket over, and tap the bottom with your shovel to release the cone.

**2**

Stack several cones to make each serpent coil. Create the neck with two columns of three cones. About 6 feet (2 m) behind the neck stack, build the middle coil with four columns of two cones. Add a third cone to the middle two columns. Then 3 feet (1 m) behind the middle coil, build the tail by making a row of three cones plus a second layer of two cones.

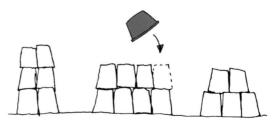

To make the head, create two more snow cones. Place one on top of the rear column of neck cones. The other is placed on its side on the front column so that it juts out to create Nessie's snout. Dribble a little water on the second cone to set it in place and fill any gaps with sticky snow. Smooth and shape the head with your hands to give it a rounded shape.

To shape the monster's body, use a hand shovel and saw to carve the middle and tail coils into rounded shapes, scraping off any excess snow. Use your hands to add snow to even out the transitions between the cones.

Use your fingers to make nostrils and eyes in the head. Carve a mouth with the hand shovel.

# Mutated Snowman

The Mutated Snowman, built on a base of large snowballs, has many grinning faces giving him a spooky cuteness.

## Hint*

* If it is difficult to get the twigs to stick inside the hollowed-out mouths, use a little fresh snow to "glue" them in place.

### ANOTHER IDEA

* Make some of the faces even scarier by giving them many eyes—or maybe just one placed in the middle.

TIME FRAME **ONE HOUR**

DIFFICULTY ✷✷

TYPE **ROLLING/BALL**

TYPE OF SNOW **STICKY AND DEEP**

PEOPLE **2+**

TOOLS

Make a snowball by packing snow tightly together with your hands. Roll the snowball along the ground, patting the snow that gets attached until it sticks. The base of the snowman is made of several snowballs of different sizes.

Make three large snowballs, each about 3 feet (1 m) high. Place the three balls close together and fill the gaps between them with smaller snowballs. Keep adding snowballs and packing them tightly together until you have a slightly disorganized mound.

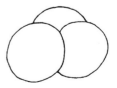

**3**

To make the many heads, roll several snowballs about the size of your own head—some smaller and some larger—and stack them in a pile on top of the original mound. Push them close together and fill the gaps with snow. Make one slightly larger head and place it on top.

**4**

With the hand shovel, carve a hollow for the mouth in the top head, and then carve hollows in some of the snowballs in the middle level. Use twigs to create teeth, crisscrossing them to make uneven grins. Use rolls of shoelace licorice and pieces of hard candy to make the eyes.

**5**

To make the arms, choose two branches about as thick as a child's wrist at the base that have many "fingers" on them. Stick the branches into either side of the snowman's body to complete the look.

# Upside-down Man

TIME FRAME **ONE HOUR**

DIFFICULTY ✳✳✳

TYPE **SCULPTING/ HANDWORK**

TYPE OF SNOW **STICKY**

PEOPLE **2+**

TOOLS

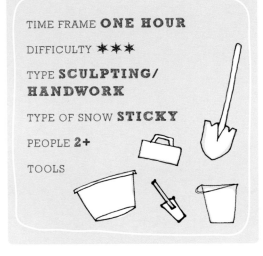

Did you ever see a huge pile of fresh, white snow and get the urge to just dive right into it headfirst? Well, this guy did! This playful and cheeky design for your yard is challenging and fun to make. Watch the surprised faces of people walking by your house as they spot the upside-down man stuck in the snow!

**1**

**2**

**3**

For this project, use three rectangular molds of different sizes. The biggest should be a plastic storage box of about 5 gallons (19 l), the middle one a 2.5-gallon (10 l) bucket, and the smallest a plastic snow-brick maker (you could use an empty ice cream tub, too).

To make the man's behind and hips, shovel snow to fill the largest mold, compress it tightly, and turn out the block. Repeat the process to make a second block, and place it next to the first so the long ends touch. To create thighs, use the middle-sized mold to make two blocks and place each narrow end atop each hip.

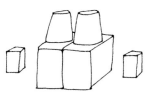

To form the lower legs, use two bricks made from the smallest mold. Make the knees bend at the joints by resting the lower-leg brick against the thigh at an angle. Compress snow into the gap between them until the structure holds.

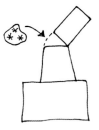

 **4**

To make arms, use the smallest mold to make two small blocks; place them long side up about 6 inches (15 cm) away from either side of the hips.

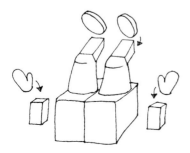

 **5**

To make hands and feet, create four bricks from the smallest mold. Shape each brick, giving the hands a mitten look and making the feet oblong and flat. Carefully attach the hands to the man's arms using a little sticky snow. To add the feet, hold each preformed foot in place and carefully add sticky snow to fill in the gaps.

**6**

Using your hands, brush out the transitions between blocks and round off all the corners. Roughly shape the body and carve all the details with the hand shovel. Finally, smooth the entire surface of the sculpture by rubbing it carefully with your hands.

# Look-alikes

These three-dimensional snow portraits are mainly carved by hand and are sure to make your family members or friends laugh as they see their easily recognizable images reproduced in snow.

## DID YOU KNOW?

A young Michelangelo was commissioned to build a snowman in 1494 in the courtyard of Piero de' Medici. It's said to have been his best work, but we'll never know!

TIME FRAME **HALF A DAY**

DIFFICULTY ✷✷

TYPE **SCULPTING/ HANDWORK**

TYPE OF SNOW **STICKY**

PEOPLE **1+**

TOOLS

### 1

Decide who you are going to build and what physical traits you will focus on to make the sculpture look like the person it represents. It is very helpful to work from a photograph; then you can look at the picture if you need inspiration as you go. We made a baby and the mom and dad.

### 2

Using a shovel, fill a rectangular bucket with snow. With your hands, compress the snow tightly into the bucket, add more snow, and compress again. Find the spot where you want to place your Look-alike and flip the bucket over, tapping the bottom with your hand shovel to release the snow block.

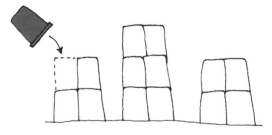

To create three faces, build three columns. Each column is two buckets wide. Daddy is three buckets tall; Mommy and Baby are both two buckets tall. Smooth the surface of each column by brushing it with your hands.

Use a hand shovel to carve out the facial features. Pay attention to the details: Does Daddy have a beard? What does Mommy's nose look like? Try to get the snow face to look as much as possible like the person you are using as a model and play up their most noticeable facial features.

Use your hands to add more snow where you need it, for example, when shaping the nose and ears. Add finishing touches to the characters—such as a hat or cap that you shape from snow—and carve lines for hair, to make the heads instantly recognizable.

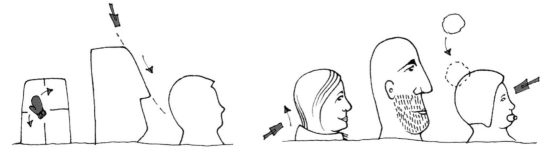

# Funky Snowmen

This gang delivers a twist on traditional snowmen. Use your imagination and make your own unique designs, or try this funny threesome.

## DID YOU KNOW?

The world record for the most snowmen made at one time was broken in 2003 when 12,379 snowmen were built in Sapporo, Japan, as part of their snow festival.

TIME FRAME **ONE HOUR**

DIFFICULTY ✳ ✳

TYPE **ROLLING/BALL**

TYPE OF SNOW **STICKY**

PEOPLE **2+**

TOOLS

**1**

Make a snowball by packing snow tightly together with your hands. Roll the snowball along the ground, patting down the snow that clings until it sticks. Keep rolling the snowball and adding snow until it reaches the desired size. It should be large (about 3 feet/1 m in diameter) to create the base of the snowman.

**2**

Form another snowball; this one should be of medium size (about 2 feet/60 cm). Place it on top of the base.

**3**

Create a third snowball in a smaller size (1 foot/30 cm) to create the head. Place it on top of the medium-sized ball.

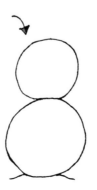

**TO MAKE A BUNNY,** add a small snowball (6 inches/15 cm) to the basic three-ball form, placing it on the ground against the large snowball to make the tail. Make the ears and arms by packing snow together with your hands into oblong balls and add them to the head, using more snow to fill any gaps. Attach the arms to the middle snowball, slice one carrot lengthwise and press each half into an ear, then place the ears on the bunny's head with the carrots facing forward. Use carrot slices to make the buttons. Use two carrot tops to create eyes. Stick a piece of carrot in the center of the face to make the nose. Put three straight twigs into each side of the face to serve as whiskers; give the bunny a carrot to hold in its paw.

**TO CREATE A SLEEPY SNOWMAN,** fill a pair of mittens and a pair of boots with snow and put a straight, strong twig into each so that half the twig sticks out. Use this part of the twig to attach the four limbs to the body. Place a scarf around the snowman's neck. Cut an apple into different-size pieces: make closed eyes from thin slices, a mouth from a thicker wedge, and buttons from halved quarters. Make a head of hair from a pile of apples. To secure the apples, push a straight twig halfway into each piece and push the other end of the twig into the snowman's head.

**TO MAKE A BIRD-FEEDER SNOWMAN,** fill a small bucket with snow, compress the snow, and turn out a cone to place on the head. With a hand shovel, carve this cone in a birdhouse shape. Add twigs for hair and small branches to create arms. Insert a twig for the nose and apply birdseed for the eyes and the smile. Hang birdseed balls from the arms (you can buy these from a pet shop). Use cookie cutters to make buttons from slices of bread, and press the finished shapes onto the snowman.

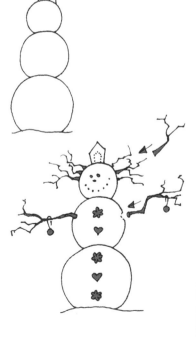

# Frozen Critters

How many different snow animals can you make? Create your own miniature two-, four-, or eight-legged animals using drinking straws for legs. Try a spider, a horse, and any other creature; just use your imagination!

## DID YOU KNOW?

A snowshoe rabbit's fur changes color in winter from brown to white to blend in with the snow. Even if the rabbit moves to an area without snow, it will still change color each winter.

TIME FRAME **15 MINUTES EACH**

DIFFICULTY ✳✳

TYPE **SCULPTING/ HANDWORK**

TYPE OF SNOW **STICKY**

PEOPLE **1+**

TOOLS

**1**

Flatten a small patch of ground by patting it with your hands. Stick the straw legs into the flat, hard snow, placing an animal's legs 1 to 2 inches (2.5–5 cm) apart— give each animal two, four, or as many legs as you like. Compress the snow around every straw with your fingers to keep each securely in place.

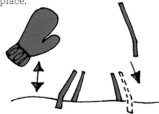

**2**

Take some loose snow and compress it between your hands. Use your fingers to shape the snow into the body of the animal. The body can be round or oblong, depending on the animal you are making.

**3**

To fashion a tail or beak, insert a straw into the body, if desired, and then carefully push the body onto its set of legs, which should already be anchored in the ground.

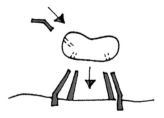

**4**

To give the animal a head, shape it from compressed snow and carefully push it onto the body. Decorate your critter any way you wish.

**ANOTHER IDEA**

* Work with a large group of people to make a snow centipede with hundreds of legs.

In the dead of winter, to create a bright, warm comfort zone as an antidote to the cold outside, we decorate our homes with twinkling lights and candles. Adding these same inviting lights to snow lets it pick up every color in the rainbow and gives the colorless crystals a cheery glow.

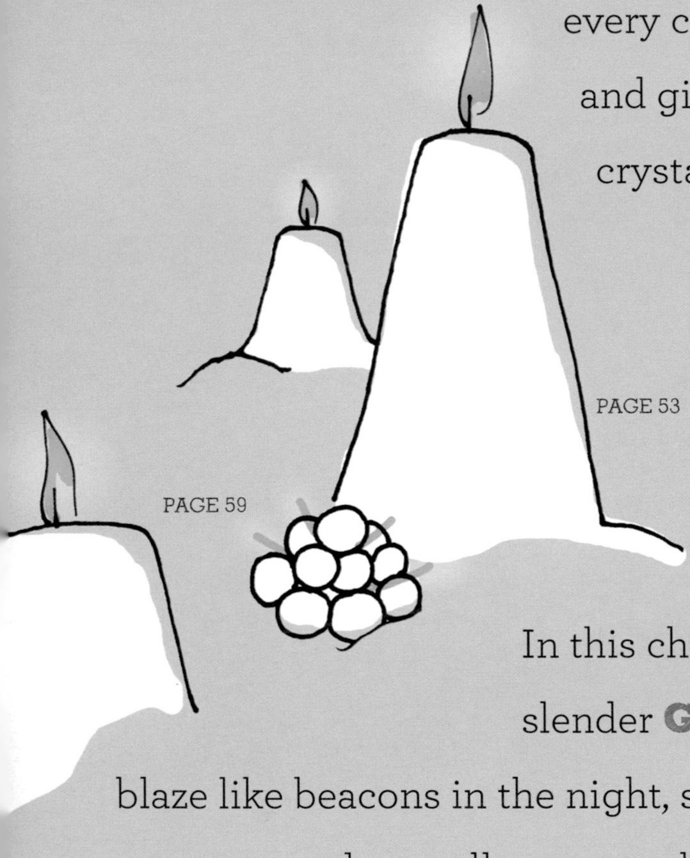

PAGE 53

PAGE 59

In this chapter, we make tall, slender **GLOW CONES** that blaze like beacons in the night, spooky **EYES** to watch over you, and a smaller, atmospheric **SNOWBALL LANTERN** that can be created by snow enthusiasts of any age and ability.

Our cozy **WINTER CAMPFIRE** is a perfect finale to a day of winter play. Just add some roasted marshmallows and a thermos of hot cocoa and you'll be in heaven.

PAGE 50

Make the fireplace by daylight and wait for evening to fall. With **NATURE IN ICE,** you can create a glowing still life of winter.

For a special occasion, try the **FROSTED CAKE.** It's a noncaloric way to celebrate a birthday!

PAGE 61

PAGE 64

PAGE 56

# Winter Campfire

In the time it takes for the campfire to take hold, prepare the fixings for a mini feast. Try roasting hot dogs on sharpened sticks or toasting marshmallows to make s'mores.

TIME FRAME **HALF A DAY**

DIFFICULTY ✳✳✳

TYPE **BODYWORK**

TYPE OF SNOW **DEEP**

PEOPLE **3+**

TOOLS

### Hint*

* Your firewood needs to be very dry to burn properly. If you do not have proper firewood, try buying some. The logs that you find outdoors tend to be too wet to use.

* This project works best in very deep snow.

## 1

Make a compass (see Techniques, page 19). With a saw, use the compass to cut out a perfect circle in deep snow; at least 3 feet (1 m) is needed. The circle should be approximately 3 yards (3 m) across; it needs to be large enough to allow plenty of space between the seated guests and the fire.

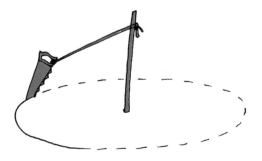

## 2

Using the shovel, carefully clear the circle of snow, leaving a ledge along the outer wall. The ledge should be about knee-high and deep enough to sit on. This will be the seating area. Pile the snow you remove into a mound in the middle of the circle; it should be slightly higher than the seating ledge. This will be the hearth.

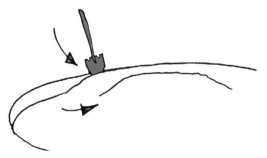

**3**

Tamp the snow on the hearth and on the seating ledge with the shovel to create hard, flat surfaces. To make the surfaces extra flat, use the saw to cut along the seating ledge and the hearth. Pat the backrest and the seat of the ledge until they are compact and smooth. Remove any excess snow.

**4**

When the fireplace is finished, you can build the fire in the center of the hearth. Leave plenty of space around the fire to prevent burning logs from falling off the hearth. Once you've arranged dry logs in the center of the hearth, light the fire using matches or a butane grill lighter and scraps of newspaper.

# Glow Cones

Glow Cones look amazing in the dark. The candle flames melt the snow, and the lights slowly sink inside the cones, making them glow from within for hours.

## DID YOU KNOW?

Snow is colorless, but it appears white to our eyes because the particles of ice act like tiny mirrors, reflecting any light.

TIME FRAME **HALF AN HOUR EACH**

DIFFICULTY ✳✳

TYPE **BUILDING/BLOCK**

TYPE OF SNOW **STICKY**

PEOPLE **2+**

TOOLS

**1**

Using a shovel, fill a bucket (at least 20 quarts/19 l) with snow. With your hands, compress the snow tightly into the bucket; add more snow, and compress again. At its widest point, the finished cone will be as wide as the bucket you use.

**2**

Pick the spot where you want to place your cone and flip the bucket over, tapping the bottom with your hand shovel to release the cone. To make taller cones, stack compressed bucketfuls of snow on top of one another. Try making cones of different heights, using 1 to 3 buckets of snow for each.

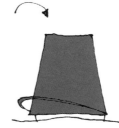

Compress the cones gently, using the hand shovel or your hands. Add snow to even out the transitions between buckets (if you're using the stacking method). Then, holding the shovel at an angle, scrape the sides of the cone to remove any excess snow. Smooth the surface by brushing it with your hands.

Use a hand shovel to carefully carve out a hollow in the top of each cone; these indentations will hold the candles. The indentations should be deep enough to shield the candles from the wind but shallow enough to allow you to reach in to light them.

Finally, carefully place one outdoor candle in each indentation, making sure the candle sits straight so it will burn evenly. Light the candles as soon as darkness falls, then head inside to watch the cones glow brightly from the warmth of your home.

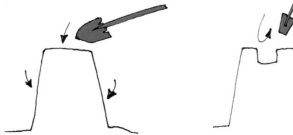

# The Eyes

Charming, cute, and atmospheric, these sculptures can be placed on the lawn as an eye-catching focal point, in a larger field as a group of ghosts, or along the drive as walkway lights.

## DID YOU KNOW?

When sun reflects off of snow, the Japanese call it *yuki-akari*, which translates into "snow light."

TIME FRAME **HALF AN HOUR EACH**

DIFFICULTY ✳✳

TYPE **SCULPTING/ HANDWORK**

TYPE OF SNOW **STICKY**

PEOPLE **2+**

TOOLS

**1**

Using a rectangular bucket about 18 inches (1.5 m) deep, make a snow cube. Shovel the mold full of snow, compress it tightly, and turn out the cube.

**2**

To make each ghost, use three cubes; place two on the ground to form the base and then place one on the top. Each ghost will be about 3 feet (1 m) tall. Fill any gaps with additional snow.

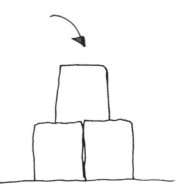

**3**

Using a small hand shovel, shape the ghosts by scraping the hand shovel down the length of the structure to remove any excess snow and round the corners. Smooth out the surface with your hands.

**4**

Use your fingers to carve two hollows to create the eyes of the ghost. Each hollow should be the width of three fingers.

**5**

Put the metal rods of each LED light on either side of a silver oxide battery. Wait for three seconds and the LED light will glow. Place the glowing LED lights inside the hollows to create the glowing eyes.

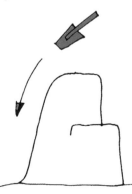

### Hint*

\* If you don't have LEDs, tea lights can be used instead. Make indentations in the bottom of each hollow, so that the candle itself doesn't show when it is inside.

# Snowball Lantern

With these charming lanterns, flickering light is sifted through the gaps between the snowballs, creating a cozy atmosphere. You can change the size of the lantern, too; even the youngest children can join in the fun.

TIME FRAME **15 MINUTES**

DIFFICULTY ✳

TYPE **ROLLING/BALL**

TYPE OF SNOW **STICKY**

PEOPLE **1+**

TOOLS

**OTHER IDEAS**

* To make a quick-and-easy lantern, use fewer snowballs for the base — a minimum of five.

* To challenge a large group of friends, make a huge lantern by using big snowballs.

### 1

Create simple snowballs by packing snow together. Roll in your hands and form it into a ball. Try to make all the snowballs more or less the same size and shape; they will be big or small, depending on the size of the hands that make them.

### 2

To form the base of the lantern, place nine snowballs in a circle on the ground, touching each other. Place a tea candle on the ground inside the circle of snowballs.

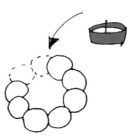

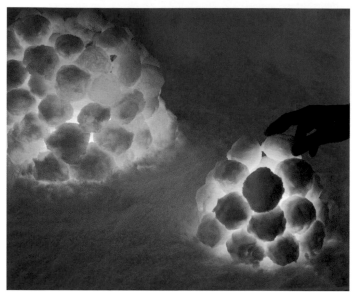

The lantern is built by stacking layers of snowballs on top of one another, making each layer gradually smaller to achieve a rounded shape. Continue until you only have a small opening at the top. Leave the top of the lantern open.

Use a butane grill lighter or matches to light the candle or tea light inside. This must be done very carefully, so that the lantern does not collapse.

Close the lantern by adding a single snowball to cover the top. Watch your lantern glow!

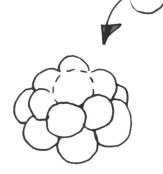

# Frosted Cake

The Frosted Cake will leave passersby in no doubt as to the occasion. After the birthday person has blown out the candles, move indoors for some real cake to celebrate a job well done!

## DID YOU KNOW?

As snow crystals fall, they clump together to form snowflakes. Each snowflake is made up of anywhere from 2 to 200 separate crystals.

TIME FRAME **ONE HOUR**

DIFFICULTY ✳✳

TYPE **BUILDING/BLOCK**

TYPE OF SNOW **STICKY**

PEOPLE **2+**

TOOLS

**1**

Choose a flat place to build your three-level cake. Fill a bucket (at least 20 quarts/19 l) with snow, tightly pack it, and turn out the cone of snow. Repeat to create six more cones surrounding a single one in the center. This will be the cake's bottom layer.

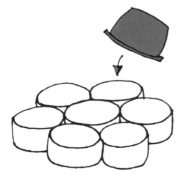

**2**

Add snow to fill in the gaps between the cones and compress well. You want to create one solid body of snow rather than six cones. Using a saw, cut the first layer into a circular shape.

**3**

Repeat steps 1 and 2 to create the second layer of the cake, using three cones of snow placed as close together as possible on top of the first level. Again, use a saw to cut this layer into a circular shape. The third and final layer is made of one cone only.

**4**

Smooth the surface of the cake with your hands. Then carve a looping pattern along the side of the first layer, using a small hand shovel. Make little snowballs and place them as decorations around the perimeter of the cake.

**5**

On the first layer, use the hand shovel to make indentations to hold candles. Place the candles in each indentation and light them. To make the top glow, push standard candles into the snow on the second and top layers, and light.

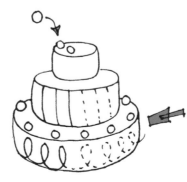

# Nature in Ice

TIME FRAME **ONE HOUR, THEN OVERNIGHT**

DIFFICULTY ✳✳

TYPE **HANDWORK**

TYPE **ICE**

PEOPLE **1+**

TOOLS

In this project, we use ice as the display to highlight some gorgeous natural materials and to make outdoor lights that look fantastic.

### ①

Put a small amount of water in a large bucket; the water should be approximately 3 inches (6 cm) deep. Place the bucket on a level surface outside or in a deep freezer. Depending on the temperature, the water should be frozen after several hours.

### ②

When the water has frozen, center the small bucket inside the larger bucket; it should sit on the layer of ice that has formed in the bottom of the large bucket. Put a heavy weight inside the small bucket.

### ③

Place fir cones, pine twigs, berries, or other decorative materials in the space between the buckets, and then fill the gap with water and let it freeze again by placing the nested buckets outdoors or in a deep freezer for several hours.

**4**

When the water has frozen, carefully remove the weight from the small bucket, and fill it with hot tap water, using a watering can. This will loosen the small bucket so you can remove it.

**5**

Carefully pour hot water down the outside of the large bucket until it becomes loose and you can slip it off. You will be left with a display of ice encapsulating the natural materials. Put it outside; place tea lights or outdoor candles in the center of the ice and light them.

## Hint*

* When removing the buckets, be careful not to break the ice: Use only as much hot water as necessary to loosen the buckets so they can be removed.

### ANOTHER IDEA

* Vary the decorations you use. Instead of natural materials, try party decorations, hard candy, or even small toys. Strong colors are recommended. Always insert large objects before adding small ones, as the large objects will hold the small ones up while the ice sets. Using only small objects means they will all sink to the bottom and not show up properly.

The first snowfall of the year is always a magical event. It's no wonder: Waking up to a backdrop of soft, clean whiteness is like finding yourself in a brand-new world. Freshly fallen snow presents a perfect opportunity for the smallest family members to leave **CURIOUS FOOTPRINTS** in the yard or to take a dramatic fall in the snow to make a **WHITE ANGEL**.

PAGE 77

Get caught up in the excitement of the **SNOWBALL CHALLENGE** or compete with speed in the **MARBLE RUN** or at building the **TALLEST TOWER**. If you thought playing games outdoors was just for summertime—think again!

PAGE 76

PAGE 78

You could also try your hand at mini ice sculptures, making **ICE CHARMS** that twinkle in the sun and **FROZEN FRUIT** to add color and flavor to your party drinks.

Surprise passersby with **COOL WORDS** spelling out the message of your choice. Remember, playing in the snow isn't just for kids—it's for everyone!

PAGE 73
PAGE 82
PAGE 81
PAGE 80
PAGE 70

# Curious Footprints

The prints are easy to make; you can let them disappear behind a tree or the corner of the house, and have everyone wondering who was there. This project is great for children from ages five and up.

### Hints*

* Make sure the snow around the footprints is kept untouched so that the footprints really stand out.

* You can make the "feet" whatever shape and size you want, but remember that if you make them too big, it will be very difficult to walk with them.

### 1

With a pencil, make a stencil by drawing the outline of an oversized footprint on a sheet of paper. The footprint for a kid should be about 12.5 inches by 17 inches (32 cm by 43 cm), and the outline should be quite simple. Cut it out with a pair of scissors.

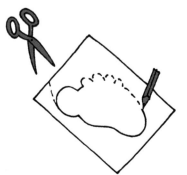

### 2

Place the stencil on a sheet of cardboard or polystyrene plastic, and use a pencil or marker to trace around it. Repeat the process to make a second footprint, turning the paper over so that you get two opposite feet.

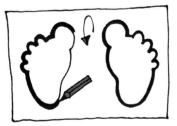

 **3**

Using a box cutter, cut out the footprint shapes from the cardboard or polystyrene plastic. This task is best left to an adult.

 **4**

With a screwdriver, pierce two holes in each foot. The holes should be positioned about the same length apart as the width of each boot that you will wear outside. For each foot, thread a piece of string or twine, about 3 feet (60 cm) long, through both holes to make shoelaces.

 **5**

When you're ready to play, put on your boots, then use the shoelaces to tie the feet to your boots. Now walk through a fresh plot of snow—with big steps—leaving behind a trail of mysterious footprints.

# Cool Words

If you love snow as much as we do, share that message with the world. Set the bold letters you create with blocks of snow against a darker background, and your message will be sure to attract people's attention.

## DID YOU KNOW?

The coldest place on earth is Antarctica, where the lowest temperature ever reported was −129°F (−89.4°C).

TIME FRAME **HALF A DAY**

DIFFICULTY ✳✳✳

TYPE **BUILDING/BLOCK**

TYPE OF SNOW **POWDERY**

PEOPLE **2+**

TOOLS

①

Choose the location; a contrasting background or a ridge will make your message easier to read. Think of the words you want to spell and then write the letters on a piece of paper. For reference, keep the paper with you while carving or make an actual-size pattern for each letter.

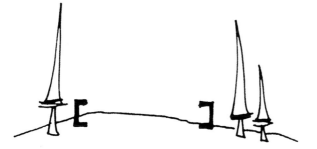

②

Using a small hand shovel, fill a rectangular plastic mold with snow (see Techniques, page 19). Each plastic mold makes one outturned brick of snow. Place bricks on top of one another to make a block of snow. The letters will be carved out of these blocks.

3

Build and place the blocks for each letter in your phrase. For the letter *I*, you need a single, vertical stack of four bricks. For an *S*, you need a block two bricks across and four bricks high. For the *W*, you need a block three bricks across and four bricks high. If the weather is very cold and you find it difficult to make the bricks stick together, dribble water between each brick.

4

Smooth the surface of each block to erase the lines between the bricks. Do this by rubbing fresh snow onto the block with your gloved hand. Working from the back of the block, use a small hand shovel to trace the shape of each letter on the back of each block. Remember to trace the letters in reverse and in reverse order so they're legible from the front.

5

Use a handsaw and a knife to carefully cut out the letters you have traced. The saw creates a rough outline only; use a knife for the detail. It is important that you use very bold letters. Exaggerate the boldness even more by making the holes you cut in the letters as small as possible. This keeps the letters stable and less likely to collapse.

# Tallest Tower

In this timed event, participants compete to build the tallest vertical stack of snowballs, and the excitement builds as the towers collapse and need to be reconstructed.

TIME FRAME **15 MINUTES**

DIFFICULTY ✳

TYPE **ROLLING/BALL**

TYPE OF SNOW **STICKY**

PEOPLE **3+** (2+ players, 1 referee)

TOOLS

Find a flat patch of land with a good amount of snow. Players should kneel in the snow and wait for the referee to say, "Ready, set, go!" The referee uses a stopwatch to time the players.

Each player makes snowballs by packing the snow tightly together with their hands. To achieve the tallest tower, stack the snowballs on top of one another. If your tower takes a tumble while the clock is ticking, try to rebuild it before time runs out.

When time is up, the referee will call "Stop!" and use a ruler or stick to measure the height of each tower. The player with the tallest one wins.

# White Angel

Who doesn't love to take a backward plunge into a thick pile of snow to make an angel? The tricky part is trying to fall down and get back up without spoiling your creation.

### Hint*

* This angel can be difficult to make in windy weather or if the snow is too powdery. Choose a calm day with warmer weather and sticky or melting snow.

TIME FRAME **15 MINUTES**

DIFFICULTY ✳

TYPE **BODYWORK**

TYPE OF SNOW **FRESH**

PEOPLE **1+**

**1** To make a white angel, choose a patch of smooth, fresh, and unspoiled snow.

**2** Lie on your back in the snow and flap your arms up and down, all the while keeping them straight. This makes the imprint of wings.

**3** Spread your legs as wide apart as you can and close them again. Keep your legs straight, too. This motion makes the imprint of the angel's long robe. Be very careful when you get up; try not to spoil the snow around your angel.

# Ice Charms

TIME FRAME **OVERNIGHT THEN ONE HOUR EACH**

DIFFICULTY ✳✳✳

TYPE **SCULPTING/ HANDWORK**

TYPE **ICE**

PEOPLE **1+**

TOOLS

Make these beautiful glistening charms and display them in the trees in your front yard. The options for the shape and size of the ornaments are endless.

Fill a small plastic container about two-thirds full with water. Knot a length of ribbon (14 inches or 35 cm) into a loop. Rest a stick or ruler across the container and through the ribbon loop. Hang the knotted ribbon in the center of the container.

Place the container on a level surface outside or put in a freezer. Depending on the temperature, the water should be frozen after several hours.

When the water is frozen, pour a little warm water on the outside of the container until the block of ice, now attached to the ribbon, comes loose.

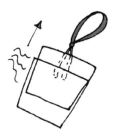

Use a Japanese saw to cut the
ice block into your preferred size
and shape. To give the charm a
detailed shape, shave off only a
little ice at a time. Using the tip of
a small knife, engrave a pattern
or design onto the surface of the
ice. When your charm is finished,
hang it on a branch of a tree in
your yard.

### Hint*

* The smaller the plastic container is, the smaller the
  charm will be. For example, use a 5-gallon (19 l)
  ice cream tub to create a large charm, or a child's
  sand bucket for a smaller one.

# Frozen Fruit

These luscious ice cubes can add a bit of winter flair and color to your party drinks. Use strawberries, raspberries, cherries, lemon, lime, or whatever strikes your fancy.

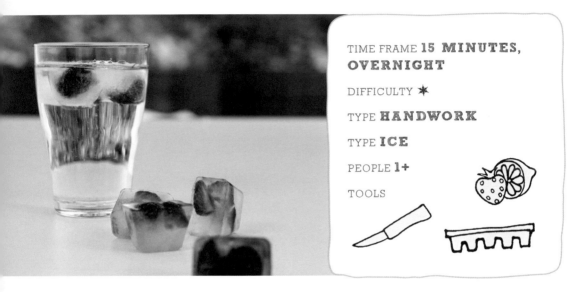

TIME FRAME **15 MINUTES, OVERNIGHT**

DIFFICULTY ✳

TYPE **HANDWORK**

TYPE **ICE**

PEOPLE **1+**

TOOLS

 Wash your favorite fruits and/or berries. Slice them into pieces small enough to fit into a compartment of an ice cube tray.

 Place the slices into each tray compartment, then fill the trays with water.

Place the ice cube trays on a level surface outside or place in a freezer. Depending on the temperature, the water should be frozen after several hours. Use as you would regular ice cubes, or to add extra flavor to your favorite drink.

**\*ANOTHER IDEA**

\* Use mint leaves or other delicate herbs in these ice cubes; they'll add a fresh flavor to your drinks.

# Marble Run

Play with colorful glass marbles on the spiraling tracks of a Marble Run. This makes a great quick game or a fun round-robin tournament for the entire family. The first marble to make it down the run wins!

> **ANOTHER IDEA**
>
> * For another version, make two side-by-side tracks of identical length down one side of the mound only. Use the two tracks for a contest of speed between two marbles.

TIME FRAME **15 MINUTES**

DIFFICULTY ✳✳

TYPE **SCULPTING/ HANDWORK**

TYPE OF SNOW **STICKY**

PEOPLE **2+**

TOOLS

**1** With your hands, collect a small pile of snow and pat it into a mound about 2 feet (60 cm) high and approximately 18 inches (50 cm) across at the bottom.

**2** Use a small hand shovel to carve out an indented track, spiraling it down the hill. At the bottom, make a hollow where the marbles will end up.

**3** Carve out the second track. This track should also spiral down from the top in the same direction and should cross the first track, so that the marbles on the two tracks might collide on their way down.

# Snowball Challenge

In the Snowball Challenge teams compete to make the biggest snowball. Then use your snowball to test your skills in geometry and mathematics. This game is great for a party or school outing.

TIME FRAME **ONE HOUR**

DIFFICULTY ✸✸

TYPE **ROLLING/BALL**

TYPE OF SNOW **STICKY**

PEOPLE **4+**

## DID YOU KNOW?

The world's biggest snowball was made by students at Michigan Tech in 2006, and measured 21 feet, 3 inches around.

**1**

Pick a spot with plenty of snow, preferably a large, flat area. Each team makes a snowball as big as they can. Roll a small snowball along the ground, patting down the snow that gets attached. Keep rolling the snowball, adding snow until it gets too heavy to move.

**2**

Smooth the surface of the snowball by brushing it lightly with your gloved hands. Rub at any rough or uneven areas, and make the ball as round and as smooth as you can.

**3**

To name the winner, measure each snowball's circumference by holding hands and standing around it. The reach of an adult's outstretched arms is about 5 feet (1.6 m). Remember that since you do not measure the ball with accurate tools, your measurements will be approximate! To get the exact size, use a measuring tape.

OTHER IDEAS

* As an extra challenge, calculate the
  size and volume of each snowball. Use
  this formula to work out the radius
  of the ball: r = C divided by 2 × π (π =
  3.14). Use this formula to calculate the
  volume: $V = \frac{4}{3} \times \pi \times r^3$.

* When you're finished with Snowball
  Challenge, why not use the finished
  snowball as the base to create a giant
  snowman?

Snow changes the landscape; it smoothes out surfaces and adds bulk to any shape. Snow-covered playgrounds and woods become instant adventure parks to build and frolic in.

Explore the playful side of wintry landscapes with the magnificent **SNOW CASTLE** or the daring **ICE SLIDE**.

PAGE 101

PAGE 93

PAGE 88

Use the untouched
canvas of a snowy
clearing or field and turn
it into the impressive and beautiful
**SPIRAL YETI** or the hip
and trendy **CRYSTAL BAR**.

PAGE 96

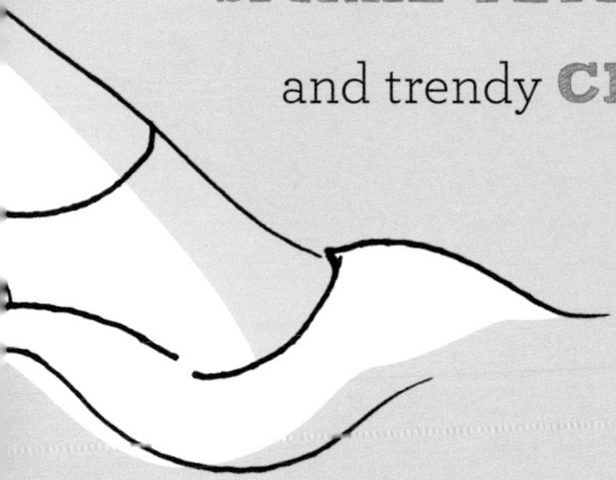

PAGE 98

If the view from a hilltop
takes your breath away,
construct a sharp
**WHITE FRAME**
around it.
For the advanced builder,
there's the **SNOW CAVE**—a traditional snow cave
for taking shelter in the wild outdoors.

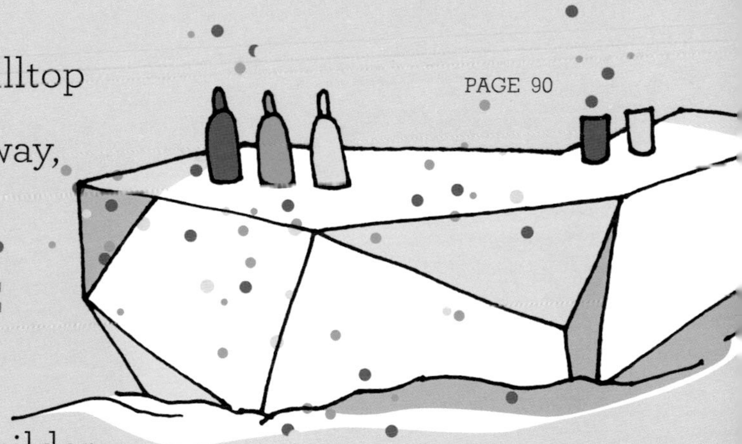

PAGE 90

# Spiral Yeti

TIME FRAME **ONE HOUR**

DIFFICULTY ✴

TYPE **FOOT/WALKING**

TYPE OF SNOW **DEEP**

PEOPLE **3+**

This project is inspired by Robert Smithson's magnificent piece of land art, *Spiral Jetty*. The pattern works best if viewed from a higher point. It can look like a playful imprint on a mountainside or a mysterious set of tracks in a valley—perhaps leading to the elusive yeti!

## DID YOU KNOW?

Snow play is a great way to stay fit. In 30 minutes, a 150-pound person burns 143 calories building a snowman and 159 calories having a snowball fight.

**1**

Take an overview of the landscape around you, and plan the starting point and the size of your design. To make a large spiral, use a wide-open space that covers at least 1,300 square feet (400 sq. m).

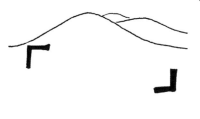

**2**

Line up single file and walk, making a spiral track in the snow that is as circular as possible. Start in a wide circle, then let your path spiral inward while keeping about 9 feet (3 m) between it and the outside circle. That makes the spiral evenly shaped.

**3**

You can hold on to one another or walk farther apart—the important thing is to follow in the tracks of the person in front of you to make a clearly defined path through the snow. Keep in mind the pattern you are creating.

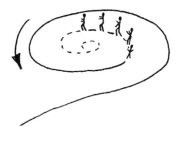

You have reached the middle when you can go no farther without coming closer than approximately 9 feet (3 meters) to your own tracks. Turn around and retrace your steps.

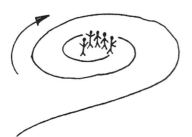

**Hint***

* Remember: Walking in deep snow is hard work, so do not make your path longer than you can to make it to the center and back.

**ANOTHER IDEA**

* Families with small children can make a minispiral in their own backyard or a nearby park.

# Crystal Bar

Make naturally chilled drinks at this bar—no ice is needed! This contemporary design is perfect for a wintertime party, turning any space into a trendy, urban watering hole in just a few hours.

## DID YOU KNOW?

Scientists believe there are five different shapes of snow crystals: a long needle shape; a hollow column shaped like a six-sided prism; a thin, flat, six-sided plate; a six-pointed star; and intricate dendrites.

TIME FRAME **HALF A DAY**

DIFFICULTY ✳✳✳

TYPE **BUILDING/BLOCK**

TYPE OF SNOW **STICKY**

PEOPLE **2+**

TOOLS

### 1

Using a pencil and paper, sketch the design of your bar. We suggest an L-shaped bar where people can be served from two angles, making the counter wide and deep on one side and narrow on the other.

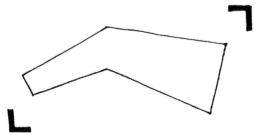

### 2

The bar is built by stacking overturned buckets of snow on top of one another. Using a shovel, fill a large bucket (at least 20 quarts/19 l) with snow. Compress the snow tightly into the bucket with your hands; add more snow, and compress it again. Make and place one block at a time.

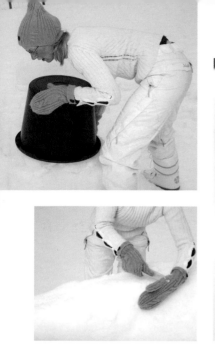

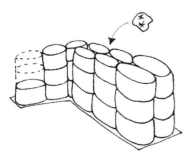

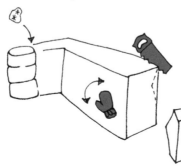

**③**

To make the L-shaped bar, stack a double row of three snow blocks three blocks high, then one single row of three stacked blocks positioned at a slight angle from it. Fill the gaps between the blocks with snow as you place them; compress the snow to make the construction sturdy.

**④**

Use your hands to pat more snow onto the entire surface of the bar. Using the handsaw, cut the sides and top of the counter so that they are straight. Smooth the surface with your hands.

**⑤**

To make the bottle holders, use a drinking cup to carve holes in the countertop. The holders should be wide enough to fit the thickest bottle you'll need to chill and about 4 inches (10 cm) deep. If necessary, use a hand shovel to make the holders deeper. You can saw angles in the sides of the bar to give it a crystallized look.

# Snow Castle

This project can be built by a group; the fun comes in working together to create a fairy-tale castle with towers of all sizes. Anything can be used as a mold—the more varied the shapes, the more interesting your castle will be.

TIME FRAME **ONE HOUR**

DIFFICULTY ✷✷

TYPE **BUILDING/BLOCK**

TYPE OF SNOW **STICKY**

PEOPLE **4+**

TOOLS

### Hint*

* Start by placing larger snow blocks at the bottom, making them smaller as you build. This makes the towers sturdy and helps to prevent your castle from collapsing. If you are a more advanced builder, you can experiment with placing larger shapes on top of smaller ones to create overhangs.

**1**

Pick a flat piece of land where you want to situate your castle. Use three different sizes of molds. The biggest should be a plastic storage box of about 5 gallons (19 l), the middle one a 2.5-gallon (10 l) bucket, and the smallest a plastic snow-brick maker (you could use an empty ice cream tub, too). See Techniques (page 19) for directions on using molds.

**2**

Use a shovel to fill the molds with snow, compress the snow tightly, and turn out the blocks. Repeat the process to make several blocks. To build the main tower, stack snow blocks of different shapes on top of one another: for instance, three large blocks made in the large bucket, and then a block made from the midsize bucket on top.

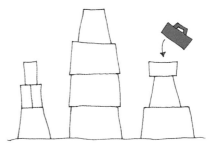

Build many smaller towers in a circle around the main structure by stacking snow blocks of various sizes and shapes to the height you want. Make the towers gradually smaller as you move away from the main tower.

Smooth out the towers with your hands. Use the hand shovel to carve details such as spires and parapets in the tower tops. Make little snowballs and place them as decoration on the towers.

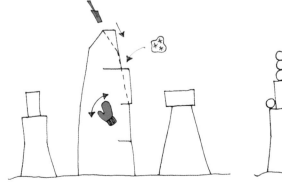

# White Frame

WHEN **HALF A DAY**

DIFFICULTY ✳✳✳

TYPE **BUILDING/BLOCK**

TYPE OF SNOW **COMPRESSED**

PEOPLE **2+**

TOOLS

Sometimes a winter landscape is so beautiful, you just want to frame it. In this project you can do just that! Build this crisp, white frame on top of a hill. The frame captures changes in the landscape according to the angle and time of day.

**1**

The frame is made of natural blocks of compressed snow. Use the handsaw to cut out six blocks that measure about 3 feet by 2 feet (91 cm by 65 cm) and 6 inches (15 cm) thick. Remove each block by pushing a shovel carefully underneath it. Use two people to carry each block.

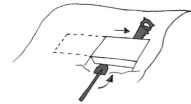

**2**

Locate a spot for your frame. Place two of the blocks upright and against each other at an angle that is slightly more than 90 degrees, to form a kind of open half-square. To ensure they stand up straight, fill the gap where the blocks join together with snow and then pack snow around the base to make the structure stable.

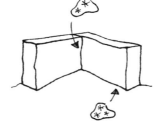

**3**

Stack the four remaining blocks on top of the first two to make two columns of three blocks each. Be careful while lifting the blocks so that they do not fall or crack. Fill any cracks or gaps in the structure with fresh snow.

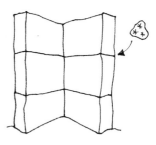

 ④

Cut along all edges with the saw to make the structure perfectly straight. Carefully rub snow across all surfaces and smooth them with your hands for a flawless finish.

⑤

Cut out a window—of any shape and size—in each wall, using the saw. The windows should be placed to mirror each other. Use a light touch on the saw; if you push too firmly, you might topple the structure. Finally, stand back and admire the view.

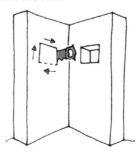

### Hints*

* Look for compressed snow on small hillsides where the wind gathers snow and compresses it against rock.

* If it is a very cold day, you may find it difficult to get the blocks to rest on top of one another. Try placing one block at a time and letting it "bake" in the sun for 20 to 30 minutes before proceeding. This will melt the snow slightly, gluing the blocks together.

# Ice Slide

The slide is a construction that invites you to play twice: first you build it, and then you slide on it. Try sliding on a plastic bag for extra speed!

TIME FRAME **HALF A DAY**

DIFFICULTY ✶✶✶

TYPE **BODYWORK**

TYPE OF SNOW **COMPRESSED**

PEOPLE **2+**

TOOLS

### 1

Build this slide on a big, densely packed mountain of snow—for instance, snow that is on a naturally occurring hill or has been cleared off a parking lot. The mound needs to be bigger than a pickup truck and taller than an adult. Plan where the slide will start and where it will reach level ground.

### 2

On one side of the mound, use a shovel to create steps from the bottom to the top. Each step is made by carving a notch into the snow: press the shovel in horizontally, and then vertically, to create a 90-degree angle. Each step should measure about 10 inches (25 cm) deep with a 7-inch (18 cm) rise. Remove the excess snow and continue.

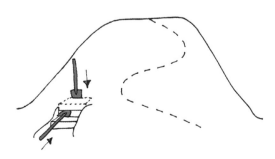

**3**

Use a shovel to carve out the slide on the opposite side of the mound. Working from top to bottom, move the snow down the length of the mound. The slide should be carved at least 1 foot deep (30 cm) into the snow to create a support on each side. If you're making a curving slope, don't make too sharp a curve—as this will slow down the sliding.

**4**

Keep carving until you get the shape you want, then use the backside of your shovel to pat the slide down to make it stable. Scrape off any bumps with the hand shovel; make sure the side supports are even. Gather some loose snow and form it in a pile at the bottom of the slide to make the landing more comfortable.

**5**

Pour water down the slide from the top, and wait several minutes to let it freeze. Then slide down the slope while sitting on a plastic bag to smooth out the surface. Pour some more water down the slide and leave it to set overnight. The next day the slide will be ready to use.

# Snow Cave

The snow cave, or quinzee, is related to the igloo—both are made for shelter. But while the igloo is built from blocks of ice, the snow cave is made by hollowing out a pile of settled snow.

TIME FRAME **ONE DAY**

DIFFICULTY ✷✷✷✷

TYPE **BODYWORK**

TYPE OF SNOW **COMPRESSED**

PEOPLE **3+**

TOOLS

## DID YOU KNOW?

A well-built igloo can support the weight of a polar bear.

**1**

The perfect location for a snow cave is a hillside or crevice where the wind has left a thick layer of snow covering it. With a probe, measure the thickness of the snow in all directions. It should be a minimum of 10 feet (3 m) deep.

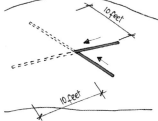

**2**

With the shovel, dig a vertical slot in the snow. The slot should be big enough to stand upright in (the height of the slot depends on how tall you are); plan on 2 feet (65 cm) wide (or the width of your shoulders), and about 6.5 feet (2 m) deep. Remove the snow to create the quinzee's entrance.

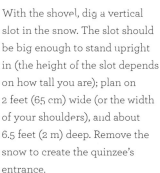

**3**

At the back end of the slot, trace the outline of a dome with the shovel. The hollowed-out dome will form the cave's main room. The cave floor should rise 18 inches (50 cm) above ground level. The dome must be large enough to sit in—about 6 feet (1.8 m) in diameter and at least 30 inches (80 cm) tall. The roof should be at least 18 inches (50 cm) thick.

Hollow out the cave with the shovel, making sure that the dome is perfectly round in shape. Remember: The cave must have a solid roof apart from where the slot cuts into it.

Use the snow that you remove from the dome to fill the passage-way inside the dome, compress-ing it until it is level with the rest of the cave's elevated floor. Add more snow from outside, if needed.

Using the handsaw, cut out three blocks of compressed snow (far away from the snow cave entrance). The blocks need to be at least 5 inches (13 cm) wider than the width of the slot. Use the shovel to remove the blocks. Carry them between two people.

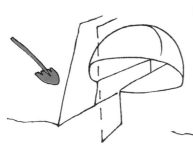

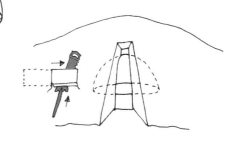

 **7**

 **8**

 **9**

Use the blocks to create a roof over the entrance slot. This will complete the roof of the cave and protect it from wind and snowfall. Each block should be set in place by two people; a third person should stand in the slot, supporting the block from underneath until it is secure.

To be protected from the elements, close the entrance even further. To do so, decide where the top of the snow cave entrance will be and use the saw to cut notches into the slot walls at that height. Place an upright block of snow into the notches to act as a lintel; when it is secure, stack one or more blocks on it until they reach the roof blocks.

Finally, go over the roof, entrance, and walls, filling any gaps to stabilize the structure and ensure it is in solid condition both outside and in. To enter the quinzee, crawl through the low front entrance.

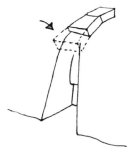

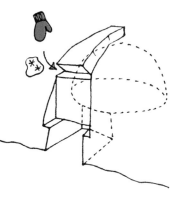

# SNOW FESTIVALS

## BELGIUM

### Indoor Snow and Ice Sculpture Festival (Bruges)

This first European indoor snow festival was started in 2000. (November–January) www.icesculpture.be

## CANADA

### MANITOBA

### Festival du Voyageur (Winnipeg)

Established in 1969, includes snow sculpture competition and a snow maze. (February) www.festivalvoyageur.mb.ca

### ONTARIO

### Bon Soo Festival (Sault Ste. Marie)

Includes snow sculptures, slides, and a polar bear swim. (February) www.bonsoo.on.ca

### Winterlude (Ottawa)

Started in 1979, features snow and ice sculptures and the world's largest skating rink. (February) www.canadascapital.gc.ca

### QUÉBEC

### Winter Carnival (Québec)

Started in 1955, includes snow sculptures and events such as a legendary canoe race. (January–February) www.carnaval.qc.ca

## CHINA

### Harbin International Ice and Snow Sculpture Festival (Harbin)

Established in 1985. The largest snow and ice sculpture exhibition in the world, normally lasts for one month. (January–February) www.travelchinaguide.com

## ENGLAND

### London Ice Sculpting Festival (London)

Began in 2009. Shows international ice sculptors at work and includes free master classes. (January) www.londonicesculptingfestival.co.uk

## INDIA

### Gulmarg Snow Festival (Gulmarg, Kashmir)

Established in 2003. Includes events such as snow cycling and snow rugby. (February) www.gulmarg.org

## ITALY

### International Snow Festival (Innichen and San Vigilio)

This international snow sculpting competition brings crowds to the mountains of Italy. (January) www.snow-festival.com

### National Art in Ice Competition (Livigno)

A competition of snow sculpting: the sculptures remain on display until March. (December) www.artinice.org

## JAPAN

### Sapporo Snow Festival (Sapporo)

Began in 1950. International teams come here for the snow sculpting competition. (February) www.snowfes.com

## NORWAY

### Ice Music Festival (near Geilotjødn, Kikut)

Held every year on the first full moon of the year. (January) www.icefestival.no

### Snow and Ice Sculptures Fair (Hovden)

Includes competitions and workshops. (January–February) www.prosjekt.agderkunst.no

## RUSSIA

### International Ice and Snow Festival (Perm)

Started in 1995, has a snow and an ice sculpting competition. (February) www.2camels.com

**Polar Rhapsody (Salekhard)**
This is an international ice sculpture competition and festival. (November)
www.sculptor.perm.ru

**Russian Grand Prix in Ice Sculping (Moscow and St.Petersburg)**
This event is a competition for professionals and families. (January)
www.icestudio.ru

## SWEDEN

**Snöfestivalen (Kiruna, Lapland)**
Established in 1985, includes reindeer racing. (January)
www.snofestivalen.se

## UNITED STATES

### ALASKA

**Rondy (Anchorage)**
Features snow sculpture competitions and winter races, such as the frostbite foot race. (February–March)
www.furrondy.net

**Ice Alaska (Fairbanks)**
Host of the World Ice Art Championships, includes a playground for children with ice slides. Established in 1990. (February–March)
www.icealaska.com

### CALIFORNIA

**Snowfest! North Lake Tahoe Winter Festival (North Lake Tahoe)**
Includes a snow parade, snow sculpture contest, and downhill races. (March)
www.tahoesnowfestival.com

### COLORADO

**Budweiser International Snow Sculpture Championships (Breckenridge)**
At this totally free event, established in 1990, the public can vote for the sculpture winners. (January–February)
www.gobreck.com

**Snowdown (Durango)**
Started in 1979, this winter carnival has an annually changing theme; it packs more than 70 events into four days. (January–February)
www.snowdown.org

**Winter Carnival (Steamboat Springs)**
Established in 1914, includes a high school snow sculpting competition and skiing bands. (February)
www.sswsc.org

### IDAHO

**McCall Winter Carnival (McCall)**
Includes the annual Idaho snow sculpting championship and events such as snowshoe golf. Established in 1965. (January–February)
www.mccallwintercarnival.com

### ILLINOIS

**Illinois Snow Sculpting Competition (Rockford)**
Includes professional and high school snow sculpting teams. Established in 1987. (January)
www.snowsculpting.org

**Snow Days Chicago (Chicago)**
Started in 2009, includes a snow sculpting competition and winter events, such as snowboarding demonstrations. (January)
www.snowdayschicago.us

### INDIANA

**Sno-palooza Spring Carnival (Paoli Peaks)**
Includes a snow sculpting competition and snow golf. (March)
www.paolipeaks.com

### MICHIGAN

**Michigan Tech Winter Carnival (Houghton)**
Shows larger sculptures made over many months. Also includes events such as the snowshoe race and tug-of-war. (February)
www.mtu.edu/carnival

**Zehnder's Snowfest
(Frankenmuth)**
Includes snow and ice sculpting,
pony rides, and a petting zoo.
(January–February)
www.zehnders.com/snowfest

MINNESOTA
**St. Paul Winter Carnival
(St. Paul)**
Started in 1886, includes ice
sculptures and a winter parade.
(January)
www.winter-carnival.com

MONTANA
**Whitefish Winter Carnival
(Whitefish)**
The town crowns a winter carnival
king and queen and celebrates
snow with contests and parties.
(February)
www.whitefishwintercarnival.com

NEW HAMPSHIRE
**Dartmouth Winter Carnival
(Hanover)**
Known as the oldest collegiate
winter festival and started in 1911,
includes snow sculptures and
events such as human dogsled
racing. (February)
www.dartmouth.edu/~sao/events/
carnival/

**New Hampshire Sanctioned Snow
Sculpting Competition (Black
Mountain, Jackson)**
This sculpting competition is
a popular free family event.
(January)
www.jacksonnh.com

NEW YORK
**Lake George Winter Carnival
(Lake George)**
Kicks off each year with a
polar plunge, snowmobile races,
dogsled rides, and more.
(January–February)
www.lakegeorgewintercarnival.
com

VERMONT
**Brattleboro Winter Carnival
(Brattleboro)**
A week-long festival with a ski-
jump competition, snow sculpting,
and torchlit skiing. (February)
www.brattleborowintercarnival.
com

**Burlington Winter Festival
(Burlington)**
This annual state snow sculpting
competition includes events such
as the penguin plunge and ice
walk. (February)
www.enjoyburlington.com

WISCONSIN
**Lake Geneva Winterfest
(Lake Geneva)**
Since 1996, this winterfest includes
the U.S. National Snow Sculpting
Competition and other activities
such as helicopter rides. (February)
www.lakegenevawi.com

## ICE MUSEUM

Chena Hot Springs Resort in
Alaska is home to the world's largest ice environment, the Aurora
Ice Museum, which is open year-
round. It first appeared in January
2005 and was created with 1,000
tons of ice and snow taken from the
resort. The sculptures inside the
museum are created by fifteen-
time world champion ice carver
Steve Brice and his wife, Heather, a
six-time world champion herself. It
includes many great displays such
as the polar bear bedroom and a
two-story observation tower.
www.chenahotsprings.com/
ice-museum

# SNOW AND ICE HOTELS

## CANADA

### Hôtel de Glace

Located near Québec City inside the grounds of the Duchesnay winter resort. It first opened in 2001 and now has more than 85 beds, all made from ice. It offers local activities such as ice fishing and cross-country skiing. It's open from December to April every year. www.hoteldeglace-canada.com

## FINLAND

### Lainio Snow Village

Situated in the Finnish part of Lapland, it's close to Ylläs and Levi ski resorts and easily reachable from the international airport in Kittilä. It has 30 rooms all artistically furnished with sculptures. Since 2000 it has opened annually from the end of November to April. www.snowvillage.fi

### Lumi Linna Snow Castle

Located near Kemi town center and the train station, the castle includes many ice sculptures that follow a different theme each year. Inside the castle is also an ice hotel with 21 rooms and an ice restaurant serving hot food. It's open every year from January to April. www.snowcastle.net

## NORWAY

### Bjorli Ice Lodge

Located in Dovre-Sunndalsfjella National Park, by the Geirangerfjord, this lodge has lots of natural charm with its setting near the river Rauma and mountains. It's open every year from January to April. www.ice-lodge.com

### Kirkenes Snow Hotel

Established in 2006 and with 20 rooms, this hotel is located in the east of Norway and is close to the Russian border. The rooms are fashioned with original sculptures. You can rest in a sauna after staying in the hotel as well as visit reindeer that are extremely tame. There is also a husky farm in the hotel area, and husky rides can be arranged. www.kirkenessnowhotel.com

### Sorrisniva Igloo Hotel

First built in 2000, this hotel is situated in Sorrisniva, about 12 miles (20 km) from Alta center. It has 30 rooms, all individually decorated with ice sculptures. It also has an ice gallery, bar, and chapel. There is a different theme for the decorations each time it is built. Due to its location, this hotel also provides a great spot for catching the northern lights. It's open from mid-January to April every year. www.sorrisniva.no

## ROMANIA

### Bâlea Lake Ice Hotel

The first ice hotel in Eastern Europe, it's located deep in the Făgăraş Mountains. Due to its location approximately 6,560 feet (2,000 m) above sea level, you can only access it via a cable car. It has a more exclusive feel than many other ice hotels as it only has 10 rooms, and every year it is completely rebuilt to give it a unique look. The hotel is open from December until the end of April. www.icehotelromania.com/romania/

## SWEDEN

### The Ice Hotel

Located in the village of Jukkasjärvi, about 10 miles (17 km) from Kiruna, it was the first ever snow hotel—the original was built in 1990—and it is also the largest with more than 80 rooms. It is made using ice from the river Torne, which is next to the hotel. Every year many international ice artists visit the hotel to create different rooms and even an ice church where you can get married. It's open from December to April every year. www.icehotel.com

# IGLOO HOTELS

There are several igloo villages all owned by the same company, Iglu Dorf. They are all open from the end of December through April each year. www.iglu-dorf.com

## ANDORRA

### Grandvalira

This igloo village is located 7,545 feet (2,300 m) above sea level and also has two igloo bars. It offers snowmobile and husky rides.

## GERMANY

### Zugspitze

Gives a view across four countries and also the magnificent scenery of the Zugspitze Glacier.

## SWITZERLAND

### Davos-Klosters at Parsenn Hauptertäli

Includes a sauna and whirlpool at 8,600 feet (2,620 meters) above sea level.

### Engelberg-Titlis

Includes works of art created under the direction of the swiss artist Cla Coray.

### Gstaad

Gstaad has great views of the snowcapped Bern, Fribourg, and Vaud Alps as well as the Gelten and Diablerets Glaciers.

### St. Moritz

This igloo village overlooks the lakes of the upper Engadin. It has an igloo bar and a restaurant igloo.

### Zermatt

Located at the base of the Matterhorn in the Valais Alps, this igloo village is 5,350 feet (1,600 m) above sea level.

# ACKNOWLEDGMENTS

A book is a collective effort—and this one especially. The entire Ralston & Bau design team participated in creating the designs and building the projects: Dana Stimming; Jan Brauer; Alexandre Bau; and my son, Jordan Seneca Ralston, and his friends. We used the expert advice of Nils Farlund, a renowned and experienced mountaineer who has studied the science and possibilities of snow for many decades. His knowledge gave us precious insights and taught us about building complex projects such as the Snow Cave.

Thanks to the designers who helped build the projects: Jennifer McDowell, Alexander Horne, and Edward Barber.

Thanks to the many people who contributed to the snow projects: Sturle Sandvik; Even Flekke; Ramn Erstad; Vanessa, Daniel, and Monrudee Skadal; Aaryan Naren and Dr. Narender Dalal; the kids of the kindergarten Elvetun Barnehage from Dale i Sunnfjord; Malin and Hilde Genberg; Carmen and Ainor Fristad; the kids participating at the Dale Vinterfest at Transplant; Fjaler Kommune, for bringing the snow hill to Dale; and Karina, Hannah Siegmund, and Sjur Haugen, for being the real family behind the Look-alikes.

We built on the following locations: Hov Hyttegrend/Eldalsdalen, Voss Fjellandsby/Myrkdalen, Harpefossen Hyttegrend/Nordfjordeid, and Hemsedal.

Now go outside and play!